James
Let's Grow Up!

Linda Osborne

Copyright © 2015 Linda Osborne. All rights reserved.

Unless otherwise noted, all Scripture quotations are from the NEW AMERICAN STANDARD BIBLE®, Copyright © 1960, 1962, 1963, 1968, 1971, 1972, 1973, 1975, 1977, 1995 by The Lockman Foundation. Used by permission.

Published by Catch the Vision! Press
909 E Palm Avenue, Redlands, CA 92374

ISBN-10: 0692509070
ISBN-13: 978-0692509074

CONTENTS

	Preface	Pg 1
1	James 1	Pg 3
2	James 2	Pg 16
3	James 3	Pg 29
4	James 4	Pg 43
5	James 5	Pg 57
	About the Author	Pg 72

PREFACE

The Epistle of James ...

- One of the series of letters in the New Testament known as the *General Epistles,* due to the fact that they are not addressed to a single recipient but rather to a group. Included in this group are the epistles of Peter, John, and Jude.
- Possibly the first New Testament book written, dated somewhere between AD 45-50 (Galatians was written approximately AD 49).
- Written from Jerusalem by the concerned leader of the church to Jewish Christians, scattered because of persecution following the martyrdom of Stephen (see Acts 8:1).
- Written as a word of exhortation (comfort and rebuke), with the emphasis of the letter being practical Christian living, inspiring believers to put their faith into action.
- Key verse: "But someone will say, 'You have faith, and I have works. Show me your faith without your works, and I will show you my faith by my works'" (James 2:18).

About the author ...

- James, the half-brother of Jesus.
- Unbeliever during the lifetime of Jesus (John 7:2-5).
- Saw Jesus after the resurrection (1 Corinthians 15:7), was present on the Day of Pentecost (Acts 1:14), became the leader of the church in Jerusalem (Acts 12:17; 15:13), and was martyred in AD 62.
- Although the brother of Jesus, addressed himself simply and humbly as *"a bondservant of God and of the Lord Jesus Christ"* (James 1:1).

If you have ever wondered just how the Christian faith works in everyday life, James is the book for you! It might be seen as a textbook on Christian ethics, like a *how-to* book for the believer. It may have been the first New Testament book written, but it is as needful and relevant today as it was for those who first received it some 2000 years ago. Some have compared the New Testament letter of James to the Old Testament book of Proverbs—short, simple nuggets of truth, chock full of apt illustrations to help the reader grasp the importance of each point. It is an interesting side note that the first chapter of James covers, in general, what will be talked about in more detail in the chapters that follow. Keep your eyes open as you go through your study because, if you look, you will see Jesus in James!

JAMES 1

Day 1
Read James 1:1-8

In a nutshell ... After introducing himself to his audience, we might almost say that James drops a small bombshell in his opening thoughts. And, in fact, we might even say that there are no opening thoughts, because James dives right in to the heart of what he wants his readers to know.

1. From verse 2, what is James' perspective on trials?

    a. Is that a typical perspective on trials? What is your usual response when facing a trial?

2. Make note of who this letter is addressed to. v. 1

    a. Consider the state of these people (you may wish to look at Acts 8:1). What would their life have most likely been like at the time this letter was written?

b. Do you think this is the way they were looking at their situation? How would James' words have been immediately helpful to them?

3. According to verses 3-4, what does the testing of your faith produce?

   a. Does it help you, when you are going through a difficult time, to get a godly point of view on your situation? How does James' perspective on trials help you with the difficult situation in your life right now?

4. While going through a trial, the one thing we need most is wisdom. How is the wisdom to face the situation, to get a godly point of view, and to have discernment each step of the way obtained? v. 5

   a. How do we know that God will answer this request? What assurance does this give you for the wisdom you need right now?

   b. When we pray, what is the necessary attitude? v. 6 Why? v. 7

Note—In the Amplified Bible, the word *faith* or *trust*, when applied to our relationship with the Lord, is often *amplified* by words like lean on, rely on, and be confident in. Do any of these words help you see *just how* you are to exercise your faith as you approach God for wisdom (and even after He gives it!)?

Memory Verse: *"But without faith it is impossible to please Him, for he who comes to God must believe that He is, and that He is a rewarder of those who diligently seek Him."* Hebrews 11:6

    c. From our memory verse this week, why is it necessary that we have faith? Try to explain this in your own words.

5. Do your best to summarize today's passage in a couple of sentences.

Day 2
Read James 1:9-12

James begins this passage with another amazing and non-typical statement—giving his readers encouragement and hope in the difficult position in which many of them find themselves.

1. What is the amazing perspective James gives his readers in verse 9?

    a. Why is this *not* a typical perspective?

b. Jesus addressed this situation more than once in the Sermon on the Mount. Read Matthew 5:3-10 and look for the statements of Jesus concerning the one in humble circumstances. Please note them here.

c. How would this viewpoint be helpful to James' readers, who might even have heard Jesus' words on the subject themselves and who were, for the most part, living in very humble circumstances (many in poverty)?

2. As James elevates the position of the poor man, what does he do to the rich man? Just how does he see him? vv. 10-11

   a. David had similar thoughts toward the wicked rich in Psalm 37. Read verses 1-11, and write down what you gain from the following passages:

   vv. 1-6

   vv. 7-9

   vv. 10-11

   b. Did you read anything in these verses that reminded you of Jesus' words in Matthew 5?

Up Close and Personal:
3. Are you a person of humble means? Do you ever struggle with the apparent "blessing" of the rich—especially those who have no love for the Lord? How do the words of James encourage you, especially considering the words of Jesus from the Sermon on the Mount?

4. What blessing is reserved for those who *persevere* under trial? v. 12

The Life Application Bible Commentary states that endurance is *faith stretched out*, and that perseverance is *the intended outcome of the testing of your faith.* Verse 12 gives the promise of *future blessing* for the one who *perseveres*, but for our time while here on earth, we look back to verse 4—"*and* **let endurance** *have its perfect result, that you may be perfect and complete, lacking in nothing*" (NASB). Some definitions for that word *perfect* are: mature, seasoned, experienced, well-developed, and fit for the tasks God sent us into the world to do. Does that sound like something worth attaining, even if it is through the difficult method of stretching out your faith to endure your trial? Oswald Chambers wisely says, *"Faith is a fight always, not sometimes."*

5. Do your best to summarize today's passage in a couple of sentences.

Review this week's memory verse.

JAMES: LET'S GROW UP!

Day 3
Read James 1:13-18

Two foundational truths will be brought to the surface in our study today: 1.) We are by nature sinners; 2.) God is always good. We have already looked in this chapter at trials and the testing of our faith; today we will look at the temptation to sin.

1. What two absolutes about God does James give in verse 13?

    ✣

    ✣

    a. Because of this information, what ban does he place on the one being tempted?

Up Close and Personal:
2. Ask yourself this question: Is there a bad *attitude* or an actual *sin* in my life *right now* that I have been blaming on God?

3. Who is always to blame for sin? (Write a sentence making this personal.)

    a. How does James explain this? v. 14

b. From verse 16, how does James describe what it is to believe otherwise?

c. Who would deceive you into thinking that God is at fault for your temptation to sin?

Blame shifting and finger pointing have become so common in our day that the most atrocious crimes are not only blamed on others (I had a bad childhood, etc.), but those excuses are even given credibility in our court system today. We are so afraid to take responsibility for our actions that we have become afraid to make others responsible for theirs! But that fact doesn't change the reality that *before God* we are each one responsible for our sin. Our courts may not hold us responsible for our sin—but God does!

4. Using the process of birth as an illustration, verse 15 gives a graphic description of the downward spiral of sin. Use this illustration to explain the seriousness of our evil desires.

   a. How does Romans 6:23a confirm this?

   b. What great word of hope does this same verse give (Romans 6:23b)?

5. Does God desire *good* for you or *evil*? Explain yourself using Romans 6:23b and James 1:17-18 for your answer.

Do you really believe this? Do you believe that all good things are from God? Do you believe that He only and always does good? Do you believe that He only wants good *for you*? This is God's truth! Believe it! And know that it is the enemy of your soul that would have you to believe otherwise.

6. Do your best to summarize today's passage in a couple of sentences.

Review this week's memory verse.

Day 4
Read James 1:19-27

James begins and ends this passage with thoughts about our speech, but the heart of the passage is actually the importance of our *living out*, through obedience, the Word of God. First it is important that we *receive* the Word (verse 21), then it is important that we *respond* to the Word (verse 22).

1. What is James' perspective on our speech? v. 19

   a. Is James' way your usual way? What is your usual way?

JAMES 1

    b. Why should we follow this formula? v. 20

2. What are we to *eliminate* from our lives? v. 21

    a. What are we to *add* to our lives? How are we to receive it and why? v. 21

    b. How does eliminating sin and truly *receiving* the Word make us *doers* of the Word and not hearers only?

Up Close and Personal:

3. In essence, verse 21 is telling us to eliminate those things which are *hindrances* to our spiritual growth—getting rid of anything and everything in our life that brings displeasure to God. Is there something that has come to your attention today that is a hindrance to your spiritual growth? Make the decision to eliminate it *right now*, thereby proving yourself a doer of the Word and not a hearer only!

Although we most often apply the words in verse 19 (about being quick to hear) to the way we listen to others, it is probable that James is speaking primarily of our being quick to hear the word of truth (verse 18).

    a. What picture does James paint of the one who *hears* only? vv. 23-24

4. Do you ever have a problem like this—looking into the Word, seeing the reality about yourself, but walking away, forgetting what you saw, and continuing to do things the way you always have? Verse 25 gives the answer to this dilemma:

In a word or two...

   ✣ What is the *law* (the Word) called?

   ✣ How are we to approach this law (2 ways)?

   ✣ What are we *not* to be?

   ✣ What *are* we to be?

   ✣ What will be the result?

5. What 3 important things prove that we are *doers of the Word*? vv. 26-27

   ✣

   ✣

   ✣

   a. Is there anything in this list that you are missing?

6. Do your best to summarize today's passage in a couple of sentences.

JAMES 1

Day 5
Overview of James 1

Today we will be looking at the passage we have studied this week as a whole. The goal is to find the main lessons the Lord has for us from this chapter. Don't worry about being clever or profound—just do your best!

Find the Facts...

1. See if you can state the *content* of this week's passage in a couple of sentences. You can use your daily summary statements to help you come up with one main theme or summary of the chapter. (Who is speaking, what is taking place, what is the main subject?)

Look for the Heart...

2. What do you think is the main *lesson* of this chapter? (What spiritual truths are taught here? Look for a command, a word of exhortation, a promise, etc.)

Hear Him Speak...

3. Look for a *personal application* from the content of this chapter. It should come from the lesson you got from the chapter (question 2). How will you apply the lesson to yourself?

4. Was there a particular verse that ministered to you this week? What was it and how did it minister to you?

5. Write out your memory verse *from memory*!

Notes

JAMES 2

In a nutshell ... As has already been noted, James' letter was not only relevant to the first century believer but it is every bit as relevant to the Christian today. The ills of the culture of the day in which James wrote are the ills of the culture of our day; we see this clearly in the second chapter of James. Consider this question: What do we, in general, use as the *markers* of recognition, importance, and even potential for success? Do we most often consider the *heart* or do we all too often consider the more outward things such as profession, social standing, possessions, and wealth? Do we look beyond that which is visually apparent, or do we, as a society, and even as a church, look only at that which can be seen with the eye? In this chapter, James is calling us to follow the example of Christ. Considering those who were His first followers and, in particular, those who were His *closest* followers, we can see that He abstained from playing favorites and, instead, entrusted Himself to the predominantly lowly, in whom He saw the inner potential of greatness. One last question: Is greatness found in what we drive or wear, or in what we are on the inside? Let us be sure that we act in accordance with how we answer that question.

JAMES 2

Day 1
Read James 2:1-7

1. State James' perspective on partiality (or favoritism, NASB) from verse 1.

   a. Without thinking any further than this, see if you can share how *faith in Jesus* would be in direct opposition to personal favoritism?

2. To help get his point across, James uses an example—perhaps one he had even witnessed with his own eyes. In his illustration:

✣ What was the response to the one dressed in fine clothing?

✣ What was the response to the one in dirty clothes?

   a. Let's be honest—have you ever responded in a similar way? If your answer is yes, see if you can think of a few reasons why you may have done this (dig deep!).

3. What are we doing when we respond to someone merely on the basis of outward appearance? Use both verse 4 and verse 6a for your answer.

a. From the following verses, share how James points out the folly of venerating the rich at the expense of the poor.

verse 5

verse 6b

verse 7

Verse 5 is especially important in that it points out the fact that God has chosen the poor of this world to be rich in faith and heirs of His kingdom. Although richness of faith and eternal life in the kingdom of God is available to everyone, it seems that the poor of this world are often those who most take advantage of all that has been offered. We are reminded again of the teaching of Jesus on this point—Luke quotes Him this way, "Blessed are you who are poor, for yours is the kingdom of God" (Luke 6:20).

Listen to Jesus:
- ✣ How do we see the ministry of Jesus to the poor in these verses? Matthew 11:5; Luke 4:18

- ✣ What was His attitude toward everyone? Matthew 22:16

- ✣ What statement did He make about the rich? Matthew 19:24

- ✣ Why do you think this statement is true?

✤ Because of all this, on what should you base your judgment of others?

✤ How is this in keeping with God's judgment? 1 Samuel 16:7 (Look at this verse in the NLT, if you have it—it's great!)

Memory Verse: *"For the Lord does not see as man sees, for man looks at the outward appearance, but the Lord looks at the heart."* 1 Samuel 16:7b

4. Do your best to summarize today's passage in a couple of sentences.

Day 2
Read James 2:8-13

1. In general, what perspective on *favoritism* does James give in our passage today? v. 9

    a. What perspective on the *law* does James give in these verses? vv. 10-11

2. James begins by speaking of the *royal law*. Look at Leviticus 19:18 and quote this law as it was originally given.

a. In Matthew 22, Jesus makes this law His own by combining it with another. Read verses 36-40 and answer these questions:

✣ From verse 36, what is the question He is responding to?

✣ What two laws did He give in answer to this question?

✣ What summary statement about these laws did He make? v. 40

✣ Explain how in the keeping these two commandments, all of law would be kept.

✣ How would fulfilling the *royal law* keep you from committing the sin of favoritism?

James makes a strong statement in this passage in saying that in breaking any law of God, even a law that we might make light of (favoritism was very likely then—and even now—not thought of as a sin at all) we are, in effect, guilty of breaking them all. From James' treatment of our responsibility to the law, we recognize that we are allowed no *special indulgences* in the area of sin. Inconsistent obedience is not obedience—total obedience is the key. Does James think that we are perfect or will ever be perfect? No! That is not the expectation. The expectation is that we will not excuse a sin such as favoritism as if it were okay because we are doing other things right.

Up close and personal:
Is there something that you have allowed in your life, wrongly thinking that you are okay because of your obedience in other areas or because you think *it isn't that bad*? What is James word to *you* today?

3. We've received the reproof; let's consider the remedy. Share from the following verses a couple of words that describe what *you* can do.

1 John 1:9

James 2:8

James 2:12

James 2:13

4. Do your best to summarize today's passage in a couple of sentences.

Review this week's memory verse.

Day 3
Read James 2:14-17

This passage has been seen by some as a contradiction to the teachings of Paul. James and Paul emphasized different aspects of faith. Paul emphasized the purpose of faith; James emphasized the results of faith. We will look at both aspects in our study today.

1. Define James' perspective on faith.

   a. In verse 14, what question does he ask us to consider?

Key to understanding: The NKJV translates verse 14, "Can faith save him?" This brings some confusion, as Paul has carefully taught us that it is *only* faith that can save us. Other translations may prove to be helpful, as the NIV translates this verse, "Can *such a* faith save him," and the NASB asks, "Can *that* faith save him," speaking of the faith that is not followed by works.

   b. Consider the point about *that faith* that James is trying to make here:

   ✣ Does he think that a person with *that* kind of faith is truly a believer?

   ✣ Is it possible to say you are a person of faith without truly being one?

   ✣ What kind of faith has no works? v. 17

   ✣ How will James' questions in verses 14-16 help you discern those who are truly believers?

2. In Matthew 7:15-20, Jesus gives the way to recognize a false prophet. He uses the example of a good tree and a bad one. From verse 20, what is the way we can tell the difference between the good (true) and the bad (false)?

a. From Galatians 5:22-23, share what kind of fruit should be growing on a true believer in Christ.

Up close and personal: Do you appear to be a true follower of Jesus Christ?

3. In Ephesians 2:8-9, Paul shares his thoughts as to how faith and works apply to our salvation. What does he say?

   a. Considering both the definition of Paul and the definition of James:

   ✢ What does Paul want to make sure we know?

   ✢ What does James want to make sure we know?

4. Do your best to summarize today's passage in a couple of sentences.

Review this week's memory verse.

Day 4
Read James 2:18-26

In today's passage, James continues to make his case that faith and works are inseparable. We will again be considering the words of Paul, as we continue our study today.

JAMES: LET'S GROW UP!

1. What argument does James imagine someone making to his point in this passage? v. 18a

    a. What is his response? v. 18b

    b. What is he trying to say?

    c. How does James use demons to make his point that *believing alone* (faith without works) is not enough? Try to explain what James is saying here in your own words.

2. James uses Old Testament believers to reinforce his point:

    a. What action did Abraham take that proved his faith? v. 21b (See Genesis 22:1-18.)

    b. What action did Rahab take that proved her faith? v. 25b (See Joshua 2:1-15.)

    c. What conclusion does James make from these actions? vv. 21a, 25a

    d. How does James describe what he sees taking place when Abraham offered up his son? v. 22

e. What does he consider the result of Abraham's faith and works in action? v. 23

Paul uses this exact quote from Genesis 15:6 to prove that Abraham was justified by *faith* in Romans 4:1-3. James considers Abraham's *actions* as fulfilling the word spoken in Gen. 15:6. Both are right! The Ryrie Study Bible puts it this way: "Abraham's justification in Paul's sense is recorded in Genesis 15:6; Abraham's justification in James's sense took place 30 or more years later in the patriarch's crowning act of obedience in offering Isaac (Genesis 22). By this act he proved the reality of his Genesis 15 faith."

3. To summarize the teachings of Paul on justification by *faith* and James on justification by *works*, answer these two questions:

✤ How are you justified by your *faith* (in whom are you trusting)?

✤ How are you justified by your *works* (why are you working)?

Review this week's memory verse.

Day 5
Overview of James 2

Today we will be looking at the passage we have studied this week as a whole. The goal is to find the main lessons the Lord has for us from this chapter. Don't worry about being clever or profound—just do your best!

Find the Facts...

1. See if you can state the *content* of this week's passage in a couple of sentences. You can use your daily summary statements to help you come up with one main theme or summary of the chapter. (Who is speaking, what is taking place, what is the main subject?)

Look for the Heart...

2. What do you think is the main *lesson* of this chapter? (What spiritual truths are taught here? Look for a command, a word of exhortation, a promise, etc.)

Hear Him Speak...

3. Look for a *personal application* from the content of this chapter. It should come from the lesson you got from the chapter (question 2). How will you apply the lesson to yourself?

4. Was there a particular verse that ministered to you this week? What was it and how did it minister to you?

5. Write out your memory verse *from memory*!

Notes

JAMES 3

In a nutshell ... In chapter 3 of James, we come back to two subjects that were introduced in chapter 1: the bridling of the tongue (1:19, 26) and wisdom (1:5), in that order. James now expands on these subjects which laid heavy on his heart as he regarded the church of his day. Once again, we see an immediate connection for believers of our day. Who doesn't have trouble controlling their tongue? And who isn't in need of daily doses of godly wisdom? The connection is apparent when we realize that a controlled tongue is the result of controlled thoughts. Jesus Himself said, "For out of the abundance of the heart the mouth speaks" (Matthew 12:34b).

Day 1
Read James 3:1-2

Take note: The teaching position was one of supreme importance in the early church. The foundation of the gospel message was in the process of being laid.

The survival of Christians in the midst of Judaizers and pagans was dependent on their reception of the truth according to Scripture. The position was being abused. There were those who wanted to become teachers, but for the wrong reasons—not because they were called—but because they expected the position to bring status and influence. James was concerned for the flock. He was angered when he recognized the abuse of such an important position. James 3:1 reflects his great concern and warning to those who would venture in that direction carelessly or for the wrong reasons.

1. James has just spoken at length about the proof of faith being works. Without taking away from that premise, what warning does he give his readers? v. 1a

    a. What reason does he give for making such an exception? v. 1b

    b. Considering what you understand about the ministry of teaching, why do you think teachers would be judged more strictly than others?

2. Throughout the Bible, warnings are given along the line of James' own concerns. From the following verses, share the important words which were spoken by:

    Jeremiah—Jeremiah 45:5a

    Jesus—Luke 12:48b

    Paul (in his instructions for choosing leaders)—1 Timothy 3: 6

3. What do you think some of the pre-requisites might be for becoming a teacher?

   a. Can you explain the difference between doing *good works* and being called into *teaching* (or another area of spiritual leadership)?

4. James explains the thought process he begins in verse 1 more fully in verse 2. Notice in this verse that he doesn't say *you*, he says *we*. What do we *all* do? v. 2a

   a. How is a person's maturity proven according to this verse?

   b. Do you bear witness with what James is saying here? Have you seen this proven out? Share your thoughts.

In a word: Do a word study on the word *perfect* from James 3:2. You may begin by using a dictionary and looking up the word. In order to discover the original Greek meaning of this particular word for *perfect*, you will have to look up the word in a concordance or word study book. You may also look up the cross-references listed in your Bible margin for that word. Write here what you discover.

5. Is James saying a teacher must be a perfect person? What is he saying?

   a. If someone is called by God to be a teacher, do you think they should shy away from that calling? Explain your thoughts.

6. As a conclusion to the exhortation in James 3:1-2, share your understanding of the responsibility of a teacher. (You may see 1 Peter 4:11a for a further thought.)

   a. What would you say is the responsibility of the listener?

Memory Verse: *"For out of the abundance of the heart the mouth speaks."* Matthew 12:34b

7. Do your best to summarize today's passage in a couple of sentences.

Day 2
Read James 3:3-6

James paints a number of *word pictures* for us in James 3. In verse 2, we were led to imagine ourselves as a bridled horse. The thought is that, if we can control our tongue, we will be able, like a horse that is bridled, to control everything else. What a picture of power! Today we will see just how powerful the tongue truly is.

1. There are more word pictures in our passage today. These particular pictures give us a real sense of the power of such a small part of our body—the tongue. First make note of the small thing James uses as a picture of the tongue, then share the power of that small thing.

1st picture—

- ✤ What is the *small thing*? v. 3
- ✤ What can that small thing accomplish?

2nd picture—

- ✤ What is the *small thing*? v. 4
- ✤ What can that small thing accomplish?

3rd picture—

- ✤ What is the *small thing*? v. 5
- ✤ What can that small thing accomplish?

4th picture—

- ✤ What is the tongue *called*? v. 6
- ✤ What two things does James say it can do?

2. From these pictures, explain exactly what James' point is.

a. Do you have a personal experience that goes along with what James is saying in these verses? Share it with the purpose of encouraging your group to good. (Be careful that it doesn't point to fault in another.)

3. Colossians 3:5-9 gives example to the potential there is for our tongue to be used for evil. What are some of the sins of the tongue mentioned there (vv. 8-9)?

Up close and personal: Is there an area in this passage that is a special problem for you? You don't need to share this with your group, but do share it with your God, by way of confession. As we proceed in the lesson, we will consider His participation in helping us with our problem.

Review this week's memory verse.

Day 3
Read James 3:7-12

1. Continuing with word pictures, James now points out the ability of men to tame all things. What *can* be tamed? v. 7

    a. What *can't* be tamed? v. 8

    b. How does he describe it here?

✣ Have you ever noticed that your tongue is unruly (restless, NASB)? Describe how you have seen it that way.

✣ Have you ever seen your tongue to be full of poison? In a general way, describe how you have seen it to be that way.

2. What are two ways we use our tongue, according to verse 9?

   a. How does verse 10 define this? What is James' response?

3. In verses 11-12, James paints three more word pictures:

1st picture—v. 11
   ✣ What is the *picture*?

   ✣ What is he saying?

2nd picture—v. 12a
   ✣ What is the *picture*?

   ✣ What is he saying?

3rd picture—v. 12b
   ✣ What is the *picture*?

   ✣ What is he saying?

a. Do you have the problem that is illustrated in these verses? Explain yourself.

The Life Application Bible Commentary on James makes a wonderful observation. It says, "No person can tame the tongue, but Christ can." Augustine says it this way: "He does not say no one can tame the tongue, but no one of men; so that when it is tamed we confess that this is brought about by the pity, the help, and the grace of God."

b. Do you need the pity, the help, and the grace of God in the area of your tongue? Write a prayer to God asking Him to help you in this extremely important area. Be specific with Him. He not only is willing to help you, but He wants to!

4. We saw in Colossians 3 the way we can use our tongue to *sin*. That chapter also gives us the *how-to* on using our tongue and our entire being to *bless*. Look at Colossians 3:12-14 and record what we are exhorted to do.

a. Notice that we are to put on a *heart* of compassion, etc. See if you can share how this concept relates to our memory verse this week.

5. Do your best to summarize today's passage in a couple of sentences.

Review this week's memory verse.

Day 4
Read James 3:13-18

In today's passage, we will once again deal with the subject of wisdom, which was introduced to us in James 1.

1. What did James say to us about wisdom in James 1:5?

This is a great way to start our study today — realizing that wisdom is ours for the asking!

   a. Explain the one qualification James made in James 1:6-8.

Take note: In chapter 1, James spoke of wisdom in general, especially applying it to our endurance during trials. Today we are looking at wisdom in the context of teaching and the use of our tongue. In *The NIV Application Commentary*, David P. Nystrom says, "There is great potential stored up in the tongue, just as there is great potential in the position of teacher. Both must be exercised with the wisdom of God."

Let's consider carefully the points James makes in today's passage about *wisdom*.

2. How is our wisdom discerned by others? v. 13

   a. What word does James use to describe wisdom in verse 13?

   b. Do a word study on the word *meek*. Share what you discover.

   c. Who does this wisdom describe? See Matthew 11:29 and share what you learn there about Him. How might it be that we would find *rest* in imitating this wise one?

3. Contrast the type of wisdom we're to have, according to verse 13 (and the discovery you have made about that word *meek*), with the description given in verse 14.

   a. It is implied in verse 14 that the person who has these attitudes thinks himself wise. Does James think this person is wise? What does he think?

   b. What is proven about *that* kind of wisdom, according to verse 15?

c. Why? v. 16

Up close and personal: If you realize right now that there is bitter envy and self-seeking (or selfish ambition) in *your* heart—what do you now know to be true about *that* wisdom? (Keep your answer personal—what do you now know about *yourself?*) Will you repent of this as a sin and ask God to give you His wisdom in a meek heart? You need to realize your need of His help in changing your heart in this way. Humbly ask Him to help you.

4. List the seven qualities of the *"wisdom that is from above"* and look them up in the dictionary or write your own brief description of what you believe each of them to be.

⚜

⚜

⚜

⚜

⚜

⚜

⚜

a. James' final word on this note is all about *peace*. What do you think he is encouraging us to do in verse 16? (Remember again that the original focus of this chapter has to do with the tongue.)

5. Do your best to summarize today's passage in a couple of sentences.

Review this week's memory verse.

Day 5
Overview of James 3

Today we will be looking at the passage we have studied this week as a whole. The goal is to find the main lessons the Lord has for us from this chapter. Don't worry about being clever or profound— just do your best!

Find the Facts...

1. See if you can state the *content* of this week's passage in a couple of sentences. You can use your daily summary statements to help you come up with one main theme or summary of the chapter. (Who is speaking, what is taking place, what is the main subject?)

Look for the Heart...

2. What do you think is the main *lesson* of this chapter? (What spiritual truths are taught here? Look for a command, a word of exhortation, a promise, etc.)

Hear Him Speak...

3. Look for a *personal application* from the content of this chapter. It should come from the lesson you got from the chapter (question 2). How will you apply the lesson to yourself?

4. Was there a particular verse that ministered to you this week? What was it and how did it minister to you?

5. Write out your memory verse *from memory!*

Notes

JAMES 4

In a nutshell ... James 4 begins like a handbook on warfare! The first four verses in the NKJV give us words such as wars, fights, murder, enmity, and enemy; the NIV uses words like quarrels, battle, kill, and hatred; the NASB speaks of conflicts, waging war, and hostility, and finally the NLT describes our battle from verse 1 as, "the whole army of evil desires at war within you." Although we begin with an immediate understanding that we are talking about war here—the subject of this chapter is actually *worldliness*. Worldliness is the cause of the war within the believer. The sickness is *the love of the world*; the prescription is *submission to God*.

Day 1
Read James 4:1-6

1. James begins this chapter with a question. What question does he ask?

a. James is speaking here about quarrels among the people. Do you think this question was asked arbitrarily or do you think there were actually conflicts among them? What kinds of problems might they have been having?

2. The outward problem seems to be conflicts among Christians. What was the inner problem or the *source* of the outward problem? v. 1b

    a. Try to explain what this means.

3. What were their *sins* according to verse 2? (List them in a word or two.)

    a. Look back to James 3:14-16 and share what kind of wisdom they are acting on and, from those verses, what is the proof of that fact.

4. James identifies *prayerlessness* as a part of the problem he is addressing. But he has a problem with those who *are* praying, as well. What does he say is the problem with their prayers? v. 3

    a. Why is the motive behind your prayer important?

JAMES 4

b. What kinds of prayers are we promised God will answer? (See 1 John 5:14-15.)

c. Why do you think this limitation—*according to His will*—is actually to our benefit?

d. Can you think of a time you adamantly prayed for something that *wasn't* according to the will of God? How do you feel now about His answer?

James uses very strong words to identify the real problem as he sees it. He started by talking about conflicts *among* them, immediately pointed to the source as a conflict *within* them, and ends by pointing to the root of the whole problem (verse 4).

5. In just a few words, what is the root of problem, as he sees it? v. 4

   a. Share a few of the strong words or phrases he uses to emphasize the seriousness of the problem.

   b. See if you can explain why friendship with the world is such a serious problem. Use verse 5 in your answer.

c. Why do you think friendship with the world causes conflict within *and* conflict without?

Up close and personal: Do you find any of the problems James has spoken of in our chapter today—conflicts within, conflicts without, covetousness, hatred, etc.—in your own life and experience? Has the Holy Spirit convicted you as you have studied this portion of Scripture? Could the root be that you have made yourself a *friend of the world*? Share what the Lord lays on your heart.

Verse 6 is like a breath of fresh air! "But He gives more grace." What a great word of hope that is, for the majority of us who found the first five verses to be convicting! Listen to how the Amplified Bible *amplifies* this verse: "But He gives us more and more grace (power of the Holy Spirit to meet this evil tendency and all others fully.)" That word brings hope!

6. There is one condition for the one who wishes to find the grace of God to help him with this evil tendency. What is it? v. 6b

7. Do your best to summarize today's passage in a couple of sentences.

Memory Verse: *"Draw near to God and He will draw near to you."* James 4:8

JAMES 4

Day 2
Read James 4:7-10

James has just hit his readers hard with the heavy artillery! It appears that he feels he has hit his target—as he moves quickly into a short passage giving a perfect formula for repentance.

We might entitle our lesson this week *"Protecting Your Faith;"* another title might be *"The Battle for Purity."* James wants a pure church. After realizing that we have sinned, the good news is that we can be cleansed, renewed, and once again made pure.

Let's consider the steps James provides the one who has been convicted by what has already been shared.

1. James gives us two immediate steps to take when we realize that we are in sin. What are they? v. 7

⚜

⚜

Warren Wiersbe tells us that the word for *submit* is a military term that means "to get into your proper rank." If we find ourselves in a place of sin, it is obvious that we have fallen out of rank! The first thing to do, then, is to get back to where we belong—under submission to the Master!

   a. What are some ways you can accomplish this first step of submission?

   b. What do you think it means to resist the devil? What are some ways you can do this?

c. What is the promise in this verse? v. 7b (Does this encourage you today?)

2. It seems that in *submitting* to God, we would be *drawing near* to God, but James lists this element separately. What are some ways we can draw near to God?

    a. What does James say will be the result when we do this?

    b. It's interesting that before James begins to speak of the action of repenting of a particular sin, he first points us back to God, Himself. If you have been in a place of sin, how do the words, "Draw near to God and He will draw near to you" bring you hope?

3. Who does James speak directly to in verse 8b?

✣

✣

Key to understanding: There are different types and manners of repentance. There are times that we realize we have done something contrary to the will of God, and we offer up a quick prayer of *"I'm sorry Lord, please forgive me!"* There are times when it is bigger than that, but not exactly like what James is calling for here.

JAMES 4

And there are times in our life when we are in the place where we see our sin and know that we are in dire need of God's grace and mercy. This is the time for James' direction.

- a. There are at least 5 things these particular people are encouraged to do in verses 8b-10. List them here (some of them will be in groups):

verse 8b
- ⚜
- ⚜

verse 9
- ⚜
- ⚜

verse 10
- ⚜
- ⚜

- b. Taking all these thoughts together, make a statement of what it *looks like* when we truly repent of our sin.

4. What word of hope is given in verse 10 for the one who does as James has directed and humbles themselves in the sight of the Lord?

5. Do your best to summarize today's passage in a couple of sentences.

Review this week's memory verse.

Day 3
Read James 4:11-12

In today's passage, James moves on to another area in which the Christians of his day were failing, as we are today. Judging is so commonplace, we often don't even realize that we are doing it. On the subject of judging, Oswald Chambers says, "The average Christian is the most penetratingly critical individual." Ouch—that hurts! But is it true? I think we would all agree that it is. He also gives this straightforward instruction, right from our Lord, "Jesus says on the subject of judging—*Don't*."

1. How does James indicate what he wants them to stop doing? v. 11a

   a. What are some other words James might have used here to describe what he is prohibiting?

Key to understanding: The Greek word James used in this verse is *katalaleo*. The basic meaning of this word is to *speak ill of*. Does that definition help you understand what James is after here? He isn't necessarily talking about lying or even blatantly defaming someone—the problem may be as simple as *speaking ill* of that person.

2. What does James say is happening when we slander a brother/sister in the Lord?

   a. What law do you think he is speaking of?

   b. See if you can describe how our judging another actually judges God's law.

3. Who is the only one with the right to judge? How does James say this in verse 12?

   a. What question does James ask us as a result of this fact? v. 12b

   b. Who *are* you to judge another? Share your thoughts.

4. Paul asks the very same question in Romans 14:4. Look at this verse and see *what* he calls the person you are judging and *why* he says we aren't in a position to judge that one.

This may also give hope to those who have been in that miserable place of being the judged one!

5. Do your best to summarize today's passage in a couple of sentences.

Review this week's memory verse.

Day 4
Read James 4:13-17

The Ryrie Study Bible named the theme of this chapter *worldliness* and then proceeded to divide the chapter as follows: 1.) Its cause—verses 1-2; 2.) Its consequence—verses 3-6; 3.) Its cure—verses 7-10; 4.) Its characteristics—verses 11-17. Yesterday we looked at one characteristic of worldliness, *judgmentalism*. Today we will look at another, *self-confidence*.

1. In what way does verse 13 reveal an attitude of self-confidence?

    a. What's wrong with being confident in oneself? v. 14

2. Luke 12:16-21 deals with what James is talking about here. Read these verses.

    a. What was wrong in this story?

    b. How does this apply to James' words in verses 13-14?

c. What is the moral of the story Jesus told in Luke 12? (See Luke 12:21.)

In this story, it is apparent that this man's treasure was in earthly things. It is felt that the same is true in our story today—remember James' theme is worldliness.

3. Does the Lord want us confident in ourselves, our plans, or our possessions? What kind of confidence does the Lord want us to have?

   a. Which kind of confidence have you been portraying?

4. How should we speak of future events? v. 15

   a. What is it when we do otherwise? v. 16

   b. Does this mean that we should never make plans? What do you think it means?

5. How is verse 17 a fitting summary of the entire chapter this week?

Review this week's memory verse.

Day 5
Overview of James 4

Today we will be looking at the passage we have studied this week as a whole. The goal is to find the main lessons the Lord has for us from this chapter. Don't worry about being clever or profound—just do your best!

Find the Facts...

1. See if you can state the *content* of this week's passage in a couple of sentences. You can use your daily summary statements to help you come up with one main theme or summary of the chapter. (Who is speaking, what is taking place, what is the main subject?)

Look for the Heart...

2. What do you think is the main *lesson* of this chapter? (What spiritual truths are taught here? Look for a command, a word of exhortation, a promise, etc.)

Hear Him Speak...

3. Look for a *personal application* from the content of this chapter. It should come from the lesson you got from the chapter (question 2). How will you apply the lesson to yourself?

4. Was there a particular verse that ministered to you this week? What was it and how did it minister to you?

5. Write out your memory verse *from memory*!

Notes

JAMES 5

In a nutshell ... James 5 has a wonderful theme running through it which points to the return of Christ. James begins by speaking of it in terms of *judgment* concerning the godless rich; he then turns it around and points to it in terms of *hope* for believers who are enduring mistreatment in this world. One day, all things will be brought into balance. The great equalizer will be the time of our Lord's return to this earth when He will bring justice to all—both the good and the evil. Are you suffering now? "You, too, must be patient. And take courage, for the coming of the Lord is near" (James 5:8 NLT).

Day 1
Read James 5:1-6

James' words in this passage may be his strongest. One commentator suggests that in this portion of the letter James is writing as a prophet, warning of coming destruction and wrath.

1. Who is James speaking to in this passage?

a. Do you think he is speaking exclusively to non-Christians here? What do you think?

b. What is his exhortation to them in verse 1?

2. From each of the following verses, share in simple terms the crimes being committed (think this through):

   verses 2-3

   verse 4

   verse 5

   verse 6

   a. Those are the crimes—see if you can put into words what the sin was.

3. Were the miseries of these people going to come to them here on earth? (See verses 1b, 3b, 5b.) What was James' thinking?

   a. If a man *appeared* to be a believer and heard these words but never changed his ways, what would that prove?

b. If a man *appeared* to be a believer and in reading these words saw himself and changed his ways, what would that prove?

c. Who would James' words of judgment fall on? (Notice how severe the judgment would be—see verses 1b, 3b, and 5b again.)

4. James tells these sinners that they have *heaped up treasure in the last days*. From Matthew 6:19-21, share what Jesus says about treasures.

   a. Read Luke 12:16-21 and, in a nutshell, share what this parable teaches us.

5. When will the return of Jesus take place? See Mark 13:32-33. What does this mean to us? See Luke 12:37-40.

Up close and personal: What word is Jesus speaking to you today from this passage?

Memory Verse: "*You, too, must be patient. And take courage, for the coming of the Lord is near.*" James 5:8 NLT

6. Do your best to summarize today's passage in a couple of sentences.

Day 2
Read James 5:7-12

Once again, James connects with a theme he began in chapter 1—*suffering patiently.*

1. Reflecting back on yesterday's lesson, who were the ones being affected by the sins of the rich? (See in particular verses 4 and 6.)

   a. How does today's passage, in general, connect with what we studied yesterday?

2. What does James exhort the suffering believers to be patient for? vv. 7 and 8

   a. How would this thought breathe hope into those who were suffering unjustly? Does this thought bring hope to you today?

3. James gives a few examples of waiting in patience, to encourage his readers that what they wait for will take place:

   ✣ What is the first example? v. 7

a. Explain how this example would speak to them.

✣ What is the second example? v. 11

b. Read Hebrews 11:32-40 and share what you glean from these verses.

✣ What is the third example? v. 11

c. What does verse 11a say about the one who endures?

d. What was proven by the perseverance of Job?

Key to understanding: The Life Application Bible Commentary on James says of this word perseverance: "James seems to shift his emphasis in this verse from patience to perseverance, but the shift is a natural one. Perseverance is patience stretched out. Only tested patience deserves the title of perseverance ... Perseverance is an advanced result of the testing of faith."

4. Using a dictionary, share the meaning of these words:

patience—

perseverance—

Up close and personal: Which of these words describes what you need most today—patience or perseverance? Ask the Lord to supply you with the strength you need to wait *in this manner* until He either moves on your behalf *or returns!*

5. What were they *not* to do while they waited and why? v. 9

    a. Why would it be necessary for James to put these words here?

6. What is the final exhortation in this passage? v. 12

    a. Why might this word be fitting to those James is addressing?

7. Do your best to summarize today's passage in a couple of sentences.

Review this week's memory verse.

JAMES 5

Day 3
Read James 5:13-20

1. James begins this section simply and to the point and with three questions:

   ✤ Is anyone among you _____?
   ✤ What is the answer?_____.
   ✤ Is anyone among you _____?
   ✤ What is the answer?_____.
   ✤ Is anyone among you _____?
   ✤ What is the answer? _____
   _____.

   a. What do these verses point out about our relationship with God?

In verses 14 and 15, we are given a couple of conditions of prayer:

2. In whose *name* are we to offer our prayer? v. 14

   a. Why do you think this is? (You may see John 16:23-24 for help.)

3. In what *attitude* are we to pray? v. 15a

   a. Why do you think this is? (You may see Matthew 21:22 for help.)

b. Does God heal every prayer that is offered in faith? Share your thoughts.

4. In verse 15, James also brings the possibility of sin into the equation. Does every sickness come because of an individual's sin? (You may see John 9:1-3.) Why do you think James has addressed this here?

5. In summation of these thoughts, verse 16 gives a general word to Christians with two commands and a promise. List the two commands here.

   a. Why do you think James encourages us to confess our sins to one another? Does that mean we are to tell everyone every sin we commit? What do you think is the purpose of his words here?

   b. Share the promise in this verse.

   c. What example does James use to prove his point? vv. 16-17

d. Share any specific ways this promise and its example ministers to you personally.

Although James' example of Elijah's prayer has to do with moving *nature*, Hudson Taylor has been remembered for a quote he made that had to do with moving *men*, which may even be harder! He says, "It is possible to move men, through God, by prayer alone." Prayer is the key! This might be something we should practice more!

6. James finishes with an encouragement to the believers to keep an eye on one another. What are they to watch for? v. 19

   a. Does this mean they we are to be sin-police? What does it mean?

   b. What should they do when they see this?

   c. Using Galatians 6:1, share how you might go about doing this.

   d. How does Galatians 6:2 help you understand what you are doing when you come alongside someone in this way?

   e. What is the blessing for the one who does this? James 5:20

7. Do your best to summarize today's passage in a couple of sentences.

Review this week's memory verse.

Day 4
Read James 1—5

Because James was not only a *servant* of the Lord Jesus Christ, but his earthly brother, we have seen traces of the teachings of Jesus dotted throughout his letter. We are going to finish our study of James' letter by looking at his key teachings, and finding them in the teachings of Jesus in the Sermon on the Mount.

✤ James says, *Let trials be an opportunity for joy!* (1:2) What did Jesus say? Matthew 5:10-12

✤ James says, *Endure and become complete!* (1:4) What did Jesus say? Matthew 5:48

✤ James says, *Pray!* (1:5; 5:15) What did Jesus say? Matthew 7:7-8

✣ James says, *Glory in your humility!* (1:9) What did Jesus say? Matthew 5:3

✣ James says, *Be careful with anger!* (1:20) What did Jesus say? Matthew 5:22

✣ James says, *Be merciful!* (2:13) What did Jesus say? Matthew 5:7

✣ James says, *Let your actions prove your faith!* (2:14-16) What did Jesus say? Matthew 7:21-23

✣ James says, *Be a peacemaker!* (3:17-18) What did Jesus say? Matthew 5:9

✣ James says, *Don't be a friend of the world!* (4:4) What did Jesus say? Matthew 6:24

✣ James says, *Be humble before God—let Him lift you up!* (4:10) What did Jesus say? Matthew 5:3-4

✤ James says, *Don't criticize!* (4:11) What did Jesus say? Matthew 7:1-2

✤ James says, *Store up your treasures in heaven!* (5:2) What did Jesus say? Matthew 6:19

✤ James says, *Be honest and simple with your words!* (5:12) What did Jesus say? Matthew 5:33-37

✤ Although there were a multitude of lessons for us in the letter of James (one commentator calls James, *Christianity with its sleeves rolled up!*), see if you can narrow it down and share the *one thing* you learned personally that will make the greatest difference in the way you live your Christian life.

Review this week's memory verse.

Day 5
Overview of James 5

Today we will be looking at the passage we have studied this week as a whole. The goal is to find the main lessons the Lord has for us from this chapter. Don't worry about being clever or profound—just do your best!

JAMES 5

Find the Facts...

1. See if you can state the *content* of this week's passage in a couple of sentences. You can use your daily summary statements to help you come up with one main theme or summary of the chapter. (Who is speaking, what is taking place, what is the main subject?)

Look for the Heart...

2. What do you think is the main *lesson* of this chapter? (What spiritual truths are taught here? Look for a command, a word of exhortation, a promise, etc.)

Hear Him Speak...

3. Look for a *personal application* from the content of this chapter. It should come from the lesson you got from the chapter (question 2). How will you apply the lesson to yourself?

4. Was there a particular verse that ministered to you this week? What was it and how did it minister to you?

5. Write out your memory verse *from memory*!

Notes

ABOUT THE AUTHOR

Linda has dedicated her life to serving the Lord as a teacher, writer, and speaker. While teaching the Word of God, training leaders, and speaking at retreats and other women's ministry functions, she has also written curriculum for over 20 books of the Bible.

If you would be interested in having more information about her ministry, please visit her website at www.lindaosborne.net, or email her at myutmost1@aol.com.

www.ingramcontent.com/pod-product-compliance
Lightning Source LLC
Chambersburg PA
CBHW071410040426
42444CB00009B/2190